HOWARD WRIGHT was bo
1959 and is a lecturer in Fine and Applied Arts at the University of Ulster. He is an acclaimed poet who also writes essays, short stories and reviews. His poems have previously appeared in *A Rage for Order: Poetry of the Northern Ireland Troubles* (1992), *The Cloverdale Anthology of New Irish Poetry* (1993), *Sestet* (1995) and *New Soundings: An Anthology of New Writing from the North of Ireland* (2003). In 2002 several of his stories and poems appeared in volumes one and two respectively of *Breaking the Skin: Twenty-First Century Irish Writing*. He is the author of two pamphlet collections, *Yahoo* (1991) and *Usquebaugh* (1997), and has featured in nearly every contemporary literary journal, including the *Times Literary Supplement*, *Poetry Review*, *Poetry Ireland Review*, *The Edinburgh Review* and journals in the USA and Canada. He won the Frogmore Poetry Prize in 2004 and again in 2009, and in the same year was runner-up in the Poetry London Prize. This is his first full-length poetry collection.

KING OF COUNTRY

HOWARD WRIGHT

BLACKSTAFF
PRESS

BELFAST

First published in 2010 by
Blackstaff Press
4c Heron Wharf, Sydenham Business Park
Belfast BT3 9LE
with the assistance of
The Arts Council of Northern Ireland

Typeset by IMD Typesetting and Design, Kent
Printed in England by Cromwell Press Group

A CIP catalogue record for this book
is available from the British Library

ISBN 978-0-85640-852-6

www.blackstaffpress.com

For my parents, and Mandy,
with love

CONTENTS

USQUEBAUGH

The audience must be open to every possible world.
The greatness of art equals the distance
it has travelled from the artist.
All conflict happens along boundaries.

The sour hostess was beautiful, quite beautiful,
inside her Wonderbra, painted eyelids and mouth.
When the Boeing tilted on Liverpool and swung
north-west, through a hopeless twilight,

we'd just surfaced from the chaos of the in-flight meal,
salmon trout and horseradish sauce, half of which
I ate, and your stomach was settling under
the Cowboy Junkies and a read at *The World of Art*.

A journey permits a lessening of the self.
Planning for the future is a contradiction.
Art can be anything as long as it's necessary.
Economics, dear reader, is the great leveller.

The Ulster coast rose up to port, long and low,
like a glistening carcass sweating roads,
and unoppressed by the temperance gods. Each settlement
was simply a disorientated splash of lava,

aimlessly growing ... Coming home is never the way out.
Hardly worth a look, at least it deserved a drink,
you buzzed for the hostess who brought her doll's face,
gross and deformed, upside down in the water of life:

'Permit me a word; well, one or two. Just a word
and moment of your time. Just a moment
to say ... how can I put it? ... Something like this:
we have all been enriched by the violence.'

SOMETHING FOR NOTHING

Neatly sidestepping the *Big Issue* and the queues for buses
to the boondocks – Ladybrook, Four Winds, Suffolk –
and fleets of mothers who steer melted babies in their prams,
the cathedral glows Unfinished Romanesque, worshipped
by cars prostrate at its dirty feet, where an illicit affair
untwines from the ample vestments: a sixth-former and his dame
slipping away for arcade cappuccinos and lemon meringue.

He is spotted later retrieving a coat-hanger where it begs
in a bin, handing it over like a floral skeleton to her,
all blazer and legs. But she is distracted by a sudden
discrepancy in the blue dome: a bleached cloud,
undeterred by pigeons or rampaging military, hovering above
chimney-lips and slate-backs, and, further out, the marsh
too deep to build on, drive on, or dig as graves.

Only hazel stumps and blackened willow fretted over
by pylons, roped together in single file in case
they fall from their four geisha feet fixed in concrete,
with the pawprints of loopy greyhounds once unleashed
in a morning fog by wide men in fat caps who believed
themselves hammered by this temporary life ...
The girl starts crying and a daylight drinker performs

street theatrics to his own standing ovation. A business-
woman opens her briefcase to feed the pigeons. And, ownerless,
an autographed football, pentagon-checkered, appears
from a side alley like an extra in some kitchen-sink drama,
rolling under its own steam to stop tight to the painted kerb
where, from sources unknown, a smiling audio tape
spills its yards of knotted guts word for shiny word.

A FOREST

Going further than any commander before or since,
He crossed the river, blew the bridges,
And routed the enemy in a classic encirclement;
Defeat wasn't in his vocabulary.
Then, as if he'd walked straight out of Virgil,
He suddenly chose to retire to the country,
Honoured and fêted, to take up the plough,
Not having the technology they have nowadays
To get the most from the land. At the same time,
He put all his medals in a shoebox,
To be returned when the time was right.

Soon, the only battlefield that mattered was his own,
At the back of his mind – a forest
Where he had to fight his own way out.
Sometimes, with faded paludament pinned
At the shoulder, he'd step down from his high horse
And lead us through brambles to a rath
Where we foraged for greaves, or to the orchard
Which yielded up helmets with their skulls
Wedged tight, and clusters of bullets
Like sheep pellets we'd drop through the eye-sockets
To hear how the brain-case rattled ...

But he had gone too far. And because of this
He finally buried the sword and turned to the study
Of nature – what he could give instead of what
He could take, which meant lending an ear
To the ache of trees. Hardly a dendrochronologist,
But wise to their habits, he became a historian
Knee-deep in parchment, oak-bound manuscripts,
Incunabula – stuff from before we were born
He approached as keeper, watchman, guardian,
Giving us cool and empty pages to press
Against our heads but never curing our wonder.

BOB HOPE

Every swing is different because every lie
is different. I wrestled with that one great idea,
until I gave up.

And every lie is different because that's the beauty
of the game. And keep your head down.
Which, as I remember it, was the first rule.

I still mention it to others
when their difficulty becomes my opportunity.

My impatient father clamps my head to a Zen-like calm
while I rotate on the spine,
grip tightening, and my arm fixed along the club,
straight as a die,
together making a crooked Y
when I address, as often as not, a yellow ball.

This one has the hopeful face of Spiro Agnew.

Keep your head down. I lost the ball
against the sky, and never saw where it landed,
though sometimes it went where I wanted it to.

Pure telekinesis, I told my father – which went over
his head. *Don't fool yourself*, he said.

What I wanted had nothing to do with anything:
it was because I'd kept my head down.
which sounded vaguely political, even coming from him.

Remember the second rule of golf:
there are only two kinds of hope: no hope and Bob Hope.

And with that in mind, we searched the rough,
then the burn,
swung our clubs like sickles through the out-of-bounds.

THE BORDER CAMPAIGN

We could have fought on but the roads
gave out, ran into potholes, hedges,
the white lines just fading away ...
Lack of infrastructure; *Catch-22* situation.
We were dealing with computer-
illiterates and the abacus.

We had to rely on night skies
calling us to personalise their details
for direction and comfort,
while the artics, bursting with mushrooms,
rumbled on, despite our best efforts,
to ports to the north and east.

When we say 'we' I mean a football team
who lost. One was caught, two rolled over
dead, three fell apart, four
disappeared. So when I say 'we'
I mean we played dice with the gods;
besides which there were always the roads

leading us back where we started.
Not surprising morale plummeted: we counted
on the loyalty of the curious and isolated.
We darkened many a door but people
just laughed, our Maoist sea became a puddle
and even I saw the funny side.

I went homeless, changed my name.
My kids slegged me, my wife danced
on the kitchen floor, blackmailing me
with basques and suspenders.
But I stuck to my guns, even as she
snibbed the door and called me names.

Changing my face I lived off the land;
took to fogging and rustling,
as native as the last Mohican.
Soon there was only me avoiding Madden
like the plague, and Umgola which turned out,
near enough, just another dead end.

Only me and my loyal revolver –
where there's life there's hope I'd thought.
That was until dawn this morning
when I surfaced from sleep near Tyholland,
under dripping dew, gun at my throat,
my finger tightening on the trigger.

MAKING THE BED

for A

Rosetta up from Enniskillen
is saying how she made a killing
on the stock market. Her broker, a money bore,
hails from Seskinore,

while Mary, his wife, has cut loose
with an impecunious guy from the Big House
who once owned half the apples in Armagh.
I know his da.

Funny that. Funny how a face,
a mistletoe kiss, an out-of-the-way place,
falls into line
in such a small-town, small-time

country, a 'de facto statelet',
the soap opera construct
of imitation politicians on the gravy bus.
Nothing to do with us

who just want to get on with
pushing out the boat. You tell Elizabeth
you lost your knickers in some man's flat.
You don't love him, funny that.

Like a plot from Edna O'Brien;
like having a bed of roses to lie on,
alone, after kicking out the lover
who told all and sundry you were a pushover.

Half how it's meant to be
and half how it's not. The only possibility
in a country that doesn't know if it's
desperately happy or just desperate.

THE DREWSTER

When he says he is skint, he wants a drink,
but will always pay you back in kind.

When he says he has laid a bet,
the odds are he will win and blow the lot.

And when he says the weather would freeze him,
he wears five layers just in case – plus hoodie.

When he says he has been up all night,
he has been watching rock anthems on VH1.

When he says he hasn't smoked in six weeks,
he means he hasn't smoked his own.

And when he says he is 'fucking blocked',
he has had one in Lavery's and one in Auntie Annie's.

When he says he has a thousand records
in the house, he means he won't sell any of them.

When he says his mother is pushing ninety,
he means you can bury him beside her.

And when he says he would have stayed in tonight,
he means there was only 'fucking crap' on TV.

When he says he hates hospitals,
he should know as he has been in all four.

When he says he won't be dancing again,
he means he wishes he was your age.

And when he says he wishes he was your age,
he still does everything you do with no worries.

He gets lost in the bouncing, sympathetic crowd,
and when he says there are too many

old girlfriends out there, he means he hopes
to meet one, once again, who will take him home.

BARGAIN BOOKS

The postbox is bursting with tracts. A man in canvas gloves
applies a pink undercoat, then a top coat of red lead.
Across the road, those girlish screams could pass
for horror: on wasteground a body is disinterred. It's a road,

after all, paved with good intentions, and this shop is hell –
bootleg Strauss, an electric fire, the bell above the door.
*Reader's Digest*s warp the shelves, and the odd copy will fall,
without warning, on the softcore warming the floor.

Behind the counter is a thin man in a suit, wrapped in a scarf
of smoke, pulling what he calls 'texts' from their
bindings, rescuing decay, every dubious stain and toothmark,
by forcing recalcitrant spines, broken backs, onto other,

unrelated epics: *The Seven-Day Diet* holds *The Power
of Dreams*; *Getting Pregnant* marries *The Economic
History of the Vatican*; *Introducing Walter de la Mare*
battles with *How to Defeat Saddam Hussein* – thick

enough volumes to stop the door or cushion a heavy head.
Why not try *National Geographics* from 1963,
or *True Murder* and *Real Passion* to add a bit of mortal dread.
The bespoke pinstripe calls you 'sir', and pours his tea

from a flask with all the aplomb of an unreconstructed butler
poised to serve and dematerialise on command. He listens
for the bell, registers the face, mentions a footballer,
finally welcoming you to browse the loose change of lice,

slaters or silverfish: names for the same metal insects
ransacking whatever is the water-buckled, flame-licked tome.
Caveat emptor. You shake it free of the vicious pests,
flitter its pages and buy. Just right for your little tomb,

which isn't much, over the road, but still it's home.
Here's the wasteground, the sign for wet paint, the letterbox
now empty. There go the girls, happy as Larry on his stone.
And here's your place, also empty. Quickly you undo the locks.

SAFE SEX

1

He gives her a book of women doing things
to each other. He has learnt her lesson:
this is the new curriculum – the body
as theme park. From now on,
it is devil take the hindmost,
a cosy Darwinian sideswipe
at the world's most frightened democracy.

2

She finds the page, and he is suddenly
struck by her reading of 'safety': *safe-fid-ee*.

The upbringing notwithstanding –
those natural *hait*ches – she flings

herself, masked and girdled, across the king-size bed,
to be strapped face-down, okayed

by the popliteal creases on those bottle-tanned legs
of hers which openly beg

this Howard Hughes or Hugh Hefner
to become almost the last of the big spenders.

LIGHTERMAN

For it is him, cheated out of humour by life, barging in, a canal-hog,
all horsehair and conflict, gimpy, can't afford to laugh,
a smoke-and-ash man, woolly-hatted and heavy-hearted again
for the methodical locks, to be towed their sixteen weedy steps
and white-tipped gates undeviatingly to the changeable sea and back,
from Newry's Albert Basin to his Shillington's Quay,

the south and north of Orior clay, the barbarian and blert in him
not seeing you in his way which is water; a tiller man,
a coal-and-wood character, eyes dancing and cute in their assessment
of the rise and fall of these rowdy lands – pasture stitched
to hedgerows, linen meadows marching the undercuts and meanders,
all that farmland to be sepied for heritage guff, and the future

that will kill him and it, the technology and his truculence
ready for interpretation – but before it gets too late, before posterity
takes hold, it is him moving centre stage without family or friends,
pushing through and tuning in to that faint echo of heat over blossom,
the apple-yards and water-dust, the sweetness and slurry
of a slow pre-war day, and the height of an undated summer all around.

BLACK TIGHTS

Star and planet in the same minimalist sky.
Peach and nectarine in a tenmoku bowl.
The peach cannot be eaten until it is peeled.
Otherwise it tastes like velvet.

Envy then the man whose woman, partner, wife,
wears black tights, the most delectable
of second skins, warm and weightless
when discarded, but not without a second life.

Putting the depilated pudenda of the nectarine
to your lips, the stone cut from its heart,
you are laughing in the face of death,
the feline cluster of nylon for luck on the bed.

PATRON SAINT

Before language, before cannibalism
became fashionable among the better off,
and folklore a business, before all that
mojo mumbo-jumbo about the living dead,
he was this and that, in many shapes –

Zarathustra, Apollo, snivelling Arthur;
Elvis, Abraham, born-again Prester John.
A whale, a wolf, a wise old snail;
the rumour of a world coming to an end.
He strangled heretics with his one good hand.

He was a wimpish martyr, but mainly a shit-
stirrer, a troublemaker, a bad-mouthing guru
to cracked poets and quack philosophers.
A lesser god to heathens, hassler of the toad,
the exterminator of the flightless bird.

But before all that, he was a woman
with woman's ways, shrewd and responsible,
a single parent with a barring order
on the father. She gave birth to herself
in the reedbeds and grew up an ordinary man.

FLESH AND BLOOD

Gassed on the first day of the Somme
my great-uncle (mother's side) lived without a breath
until he was ninety-three
in the row of houses climbing Edenderry Hill.

Hanging elsewhere on the family tree
there's a great-grandfather (paternal ancestor) –
also a soldier, this time in India –
who, when home on leave, would pester his young wife

for something hot, like curry,
anything to take away the taste of river-mist
on November evenings,
anything to burn the cold rain from his tongue,

lift the skin from the roof
of his mouth and the lining from his stomach,
anything to make him feel at home
(which more than anything she wanted to do) –

the other home, that is, in the East.
But if pushed, she readily admitted that in a town
like this one – virtually west
of the Bann – it was a concoction far too exotic

for even a linen slave like her
to beg, borrow or steal; she who would herself die,
coughing up blood,
before she was twenty-three, no relation.

ELVIS AND THE DEATH OF CRAIGAVON

The outer ring of roundabouts, one to eight,
can't protect the houses and flats once built
in architects' basements: Craigavon's old estates
being picked off like bison, grazing bison.

On the day Elvis died, I was emptying dustbins
up on Ridgeway, pairing off with Bill down the right
on the old metal ones, throwing from head-height
ten days of consumer excrement:

nappies, tablet bottles, hair colourant;
a sequined bat-winged jacket sparking in the ashes.
The bins were getting less and less
as families were purged, or intimidated out.

Only a no-English Vietnamese couple, installed by
the chopper-loving mayor, held on in the worst housing
this side of Turf Lodge, swallowed up by concrete
and mob rule. Saigon all over again.

Moylinn, Rosmoyle, and now Ridgeway – each week
neglect tore the chain-link perimeter, broke windows
and swung from the very rafters, as if Agent Orange
had hybridised urban, and we were only treating

the symptoms. Look at us hanging from the Autopack,
our way of life – as if it meant anything to anyone;
the lorry freewheeling into breaktime as best it could
on a full load, escaping the overgrown junctions

for a lay-by, sharing Coke and a bit of crack.
Bill strums an electric guitar he has lifted
from Lord James, and with only half the words
does a wild impression of Elvis wetting himself.

DON'T WALK

Legends of innocent snow gave way
to documentary weather. Long light
from a rational sky of scratched metal, prone
to Stieglitz photographs, spills through buildings
on avenues of spit, shit and hard men,
and all their cosy nostrums.

Elvis hasn't been found but if he had
he would have new songs and a different audience,
the resident aliens who catch flash jets
out of Newark, trailing lines of coke
for the chemical generation.
We confuse uptown with downtown and look

the wrong way. But conspiracy theorists
to the core, we demand twenty channels
for a fairy-tale death, and alcohol to confirm
government non-involvement in the filmic skyline
at dusk, a sublime orange toxin soaking
the hard-boiled sidewalks and preposterous façades

around our charmless midtown hotel,
its unholy marriage of kitsch and larger-than-life
gloom. The floors have been subdivided to allow
one window per room, one light
as far as possible from the switch, one pillow
for the single bed reconstituted as a double.

The mattress hurts, and the plumbing is Dutch –
which, naturally, is how we pay the yellow cabs
(as expensive as gondolas) having called them back
from their Mondrian dance, the snow already
betraying not-so-innocent short cuts
and pernickety changes of mind.

LAPSE

All for you, hammerheads and brickies, once threatened
and now at peace, work only to music above the rent-a-skip
catastrophe that is High Street, rebuilding in a blaze
of scaffolding when we skirt the stanchions and empty windows,
the foundations roused again from their weighty slumbers
to bask in the swelter of a few more days, just as Londinium
was clumsily aired by an Anglo-Saxon mob, and anonymous
zealots inched Ilium through her nine lazybeds ... Yes,
all for you (or so it seems), Methuselah of my heart, watcher
of my waking hours, sighing now, having seen it all before
and making sure we never escape your version of the past –
the planted opiates of parades, wide streets and Sundays at
an open, well-managed fire, *The only true faith is a martyred faith* –
the faces excavated from your imploding memory, their names,
Sarah, George, Walter, Davy, nothing grand or heroic,
just those who overtook you on the road to destruction,
their sheer ordinariness making us what we are ... The car turns
a corner, the catacombs, the columbaria, and again – a little lapse,
a blank slate – you call me by a name I haven't heard before.

HOODED

Like you, we wipe faces into mirrors
and windscreens. Unlike you, we have
the same face in front of our soldiers

when, at our own particular leisure,
we solve the clues littering maps
for the X marking greasy treasure,

my brothers and I who know everything,
but our poor hands giving us away,
cracked open and the fingers missing.

That's nothing. Each of our enemies
knows we know and will gladly chop off
our hands and yours at the knees.

An enemy who wants each of us dead,
they will see us into the ground,
themselves dying to be seen as sacred.

It's the world, my friend, the way it goes:
the wrapped head and bloodied fist
cutting off a face to spite the nose.

BECKETT IN BELFAST

Bastard, stuff your cricket and oral French, your twisted formulae
for defending a second-class wicket. Fuck off you snot-thick
northern sons, so politically flawed, genetically deficient.
I'll kick the wee pricks in their *ars poetica* and never look back.
Never ever. A long time in my book. And when it gets published
not one iota of difference will it have made to the living.
The dead however will feel reborn, happy to be vindicated.

INTERREGNUM

I tell it as it is. Or was.
Driving the backroads with himself in a minor panic
towards a distant, not to say elusive, mechanic.
It was possible the white car would not pass

the test. But the very appearance
of the mouthful of names Corbracky and Drumgoose
sets him talking (he's usually more cautious,
talk means money, silence

is cheap, however I've to drive the white
car back, so I'm a useful captive), though he's not
so much talking as thinking out loud about
his parents' lodger, Billy Wright,

unrelated and not the football player,
who, between the wars – the thirties to be precise –
was an insurance man, and one of the first
in the street to own a car;

and it's in that car – an Austin –
he toured these backroads with my da in tow, only six
at the time and small enough to get a kick
out of moving faster than a run

and jabbering twenty-four to the dozen.
He played in farmyards, jumped not too convincingly
from trees, got mucked to the neck for probably
the first time in his life. Portadown,

now as then, is a red slur to the south.
Nothing wrong with that – except it should really be
further to the east. We turn right, cross a fly-
over, hit a junction and take the lough

road – unlit, unmarked – looking for
cement pillars either side of a cattle-grid. A constellation
of lights wallowed in the dark. In there (the tension
was palpable) the white car

was ready or not; and if not, we'd have
to go away and come back, repeat every turn and twist,
word and shift, everything in the story he missed
the first time. Heaven forfend we'd have

to go through all that again.
He gets my drift. Shuts up. He's my father after all.
One and the same. I'm my father's son, tall
and bald. I tell it how it might have been.

AT MURTAGH'S

As you might say, the old boy at the corner table
is *engrossed* and *entranced by* and *fully awake to*
the riddles circumscribed by the coin
on the flat of his hand, all evening inquiring of it
(as we ordinary mortals might of the Sphinx),
what it would take to remain in ignorance.

KING OF COUNTRY

Long vehicles, tautliners, transits, stay tight
to the curvature of the Earth. They follow ugly
consumption along the grinning bypass away from
the minor league cut-throat teams flailing about
on a junior pitch stapled by goalposts to new line
markings stretching out to encompass white elephants,
black dogs and grey waters of this civic core –

mall architectures in Auschwitz Vernacular
for the end-of-the-rainbow dream-stuff: Superdrug,
Xtra-vision, Texas – desire and fulfilment of desire
under the lazy 20:20 eye of a closed-circuit camera
recording this redhead make it to the end of the queue
and enter her PIN number at the hole-in-the-wall,
and get back her money and card and blank receipt.

She fills her purse and now she is ready, now
she is prepared. And with a rapid adjustment
to the swing of her bob, enters Eh? Records where Jerry
or Hank, Buddy or Elvis (who impersonates others
impersonating himself) does a Lazarus impression
in Lennon specs and Jesus beard while downpiping
bluegrass to soothe the rock and yawl of the heart.

Any old heart. Even so, with his patella cracked
by hawks in league with doves, he will never emerge
to have his 2point4, the expected immortality,
never make it to where a new pound, good as gold,
loosens a trolley from the chain gang, nor get to
centre-lock an overdesigned car impatient on its grid
in the seamless acreage of free parking,

that circle of hell patrolled by dalek police, tarmac shades
from the banks of the Styx, for he has priced himself
out of the market in this country of the lovelorn
and loveblind where the one-eyed king is god,
but less real to him than the Eno-ambient drone
of a kneeling Ulsterbus shuttling between Adshels
across this back-to-the-drawing-board 'City of the Future',

this 60s' Roundaboutville, a truly circular ring road
with sudden anabranches and fade-outs, dead ends
and offcuts, half-built by cowboys, half-erased
by clerks, and now bathed in Wellsian sodium
beneath local thunder. He counts the day's takings,
closes up, shutters down, and heads outside and home,
past the bottle bank, paper bank, clothes bank,

where a spotty psychopath has glossed KATHIE IS A RIDE
on the cycle path; past bicycles joined in wedlock
making him somewhat less sad because, after selling
the redhead *Patsy Cline Sings*, he is striding away
on Health Trust crutches (like gold dust in this neck
of the sticks), with only the look off her face
(quizzical) when she perused the words on the sleeve,

how her ankles crossed (in an X), the shape
her lips made (oval) when she parted with the readies
and took the vinyl, old-fashioned but more authentic
so she said, imprinting herself on the dodgy video
of his synapses spliced by interference and wound back
from the night before for the night to come,
when the shop floors will plume and cook

behind yawning figures, and plans are hatched
like ugly reptiles – out there, where rivers die
and chaos begins, some place in the temporary brightness
a league from here, behind the scree of fresh housing
where the rain peels off to the north, and the referee,
who has been sworn at once too often, goddammit,
is failing to blow full time, finito Benito, game over.

DERRY UNDER SNOW

for Suzanne

The philosopher-bishop
watches a blizzard
settle like a besieger
on the grumbling hills.
It drifts in the dark,
whiteness of feathers,
to thaw and float away
where the river melts,
as he melts into the walls
when nobody's looking
to reappear through
a trapdoor in the spire
of a freshly-fallen
cathedral of snow.

SAVOY

While I sup a butterscotch ice in the Tower Cafe,
West Street, my parents sneak in after me,
out of breath, not yet in love but getting there,
climbing the steep stairs to a table by the window,
my father lagging behind while my mother orders
a Knickerbocker Glory for him and a symphony
of flavours for herself, and grabs the seat
with a side view of the town church
and the dance hall where they met not a month before.

She's reminding him that although one day
the Savoy will be no more than an over-sized,
under-used furniture and carpet showroom,
if he could put his ear to the split
in the double doors it would still seem
to resonate with the muffled syncopation
of Big Tom and the Mainliners and Frankie Donnelly
and the Polka Dots, the likes of which, she says,
will never be seen again this side of the Yukon.

YAHOO

My grandfather, white-haired even then,
related the story of Robert Lundy
opening Derry's oakwood gates.
'Londonderry' – he corrected himself.

Though everyone who was anyone was there,
and the bonfire reaching a pinnacle
outside Ellis' mock-Tudor pub,
I wanted home, out of this old movie,

for suddenly above the crowd
danced a scarecrow, dressed in
black tie and tails, and white gloves,
a powdered wig flaking his top hat,

all carried on the shoulders of a local thug,
small and hateful, a two-headed throwback
pushing children over pallets,
bald tyres and dead cats dowsed in petrol.

'Won't they burn him soon?'
'Soon,' my grandfather replied, above my head
and holding my little hand tighter,
not prepared to give anything away.

‘And will they close the gates?’
‘Now there’s a question, son –
We’ll have to wait and see.’ He bent down
and grinned: ‘Let’s wait and see.’

CALDERA

The orange of the target flag fluttering
against a sea of green. Laughter and the choice
of clubs, the spark of a putter hitting par.

⋆

Tractors stitch the distance into a grey net
beneath flat-bottomed clouds moored
in the shallows of the sky above south Armagh.

⋆

The broadcast media and army who eavesdrop
from the high ground of this carious crater
have the eyes and hearts of hermits.

⋆

Ah, voyeurs! The walk ahead is already known
to those who listen to the air
as is the walk back far from where we were.

STATESIDE

Down the Connemara Approaches, high and bright and fat
with shadow water, the cloud armada reaches Spanish Point
where – out of madness or spite, the crew capricious
or *el capitano* venal – one of its number throws a wobbly
and strikes out west (not wholly unknown territory,
but strange nonetheless) taking several weeks to cross
the Atlantic, gatecrashing the fog banks of Labrador,
Vinland, fishy New Scotland, the Arcadian glitter,
before turning south over freighters and trawlers, seabirds
spread-eagled on sea air, to haul up, depleted, out of steam,
dropping anchor as a shower of rain on the surprised heads
of tourists crowding the glass island turret of the Empire State
who just happen to be photographing, at that moment,
the shallows of what is, from there, a parched Manhattan.

NAVAN

Stop it, you're looking at history.
A bit of respect please: lower your voice,
wipe your feet – this was history
before your family even had a name.
So please don't judge, for history
has given us this grass to eat.

In their day the world was flat.
They fought here, pissed and steadied
themselves on their own two feet
after a night's session. And
listen, Ptolemy was here before that,
and God knows who else besides,

gave the land a name (good or bad
it's still a name), the Barbary ape swung
ashore and climbed a tree
to catch sight of home,
but all it got was Slemish, Croob,
the brown hills of Armagh and Tyrone.

They must have been a fit lot to climb
this slope of umbellifers,
fresh as a daisy, finding the time
to kill a few hours. An easy life
I could warm to, but not your scene;
then there are the day-trippers –

a rust-bucket pulling up, nuclear family
falling out with sister nun in tow,
to visit where sultry Macha gave birth.
It's no use, you've sex on the brain;
no change, you've blood on your hands.
I give in: here, wipe them on this lump of turf.

THE CAMBER

Watching the man who paints the white lines
along the middle of the road – old, new, reopened
or repaired, between upturned soil and the death
of fields – maybe I am that man, head down,

one eye on the camber, the other on his splattered
shoes and turn-ups, the scuffed toecaps,
a smoking lorry in his wake as he pushes
the trolley of bubbling paint with all the slowness

of a surgeon having the miles cut out for him
by a stencil giving the paint a straight edge,
and him knowing because of some gauge
or environmental plan when to dot and when to dash

or go unbroken on the long dangerous curves,
so keeping both sides apart by not being there –
though nothing in himself – a balancing act
of how to leave even the simplest mark.

LAST LOOK

The old man asks for money
simply because you have taken his wife.
You refuse, and load another roll of Ektachrome.
These people are like kilometres –
again we're on the wrong side of the road.

After a late breakfast we leave
the scalding zinc-top and head down to the oven
of the rental car, frowned on by gawky geraniums
lining the awkward steps, creased
like silver pillows below the Alhambra

tricked out in unfaltering light
and a good crick of the neck from our parking space.
Perspective makes a difference to our viewpoint
so we add to it our calculations,
and up we go, if only to see

how far we have come from the winter tiger
of the Sierra Nevada stalking this city and plain,
its striped haunches flexed to realign
the muscular snow. At which point,
like homesick Moors,

we agree that this last look is as seductive
as the first; except, when we look again,
the hermetic rooftops and tesserae of agriculture,
too late, it's already lost to us, the last province
to fall to the poor envious Christians.

ST PADDY'S

We promise as all lovers do, sooner or later,
to get drunk in the afternoon while it's still
bright and optimistic and dizzy-making,
to pub-crawl in one tremendous eccentric
circle of glam retro bars, re-themed grocers
and recycled churchy-cool interiors, loud
and woody, beer-bottled, clattery, a tunnel
of shocks and pleasures, brand names made
fashionable all over again, multi-levels
of smoke-heavy stairwells and balconies
crammed with music I loved the first time round,
but now feel too young for, danced-out,
too quiet, still preternaturally shy
(though as with all these things I was told
I would grow out of it eventually),
our dead glasses left behind for bar staff
half our age, the waitresses like cryptic
egg timers, tuning forks, all waistline
and sober chignons, filling their time
on hormonal smiles when we leave
the manufactured dark for natural pubs of two,
three drinkers who see and cry but can't talk,
names like Lynchechaun, No-Belly and Glasker,
spokes on that great gently-turning wheel
rolling us back double-handed to the beginning
under Carmichael stars and Yankee neon,

and emotions that have never been put to bed
in all our years, as if we were only passing
through like everyone else that day
and counting what we could take with us.

THIS FAR AWAY

Absolutes of water and atmosphere wait for us
across barbed wire, the distance rubbed flat, and the rustle
of waves held by the cave's cold-collecting dark.

Raffish, roof-high vertical sheep. A gargle of seagulls
against the grain of dunes; a turquoise sea caught
in every dip and cut between rough land and gables ...

A cat pours itself over a wall. A canny dog adopts
and trails us like a dangerous thought we want forgotten.
It turns out the sky is one of two things, a Magritte
or a blue and white cow. But such interruptions are rare

because we think this far away nothing will happen,
yet when we get there we are different – brash, louder,
more flush, less impatient – with enough to drink
and space to roam and never retrace our conjoined steps.

THE BRACELET

Fanned out, lark-risers, men and boys fishing
along the parapet of a long low bridge,
all morning landing this and that, when one son
sniggles something furious on the riverbed,
a deep feeder, heavy, a live wire raging against
its torrential luck (for it's a secular fish),
the boy reeling back, rapidly freezing,
dragging its weight in slow motion then giving slack,
then letting go, allowing the fierce catch
to drive forward thinking itself free (an idealistic fish),
only for him to reel and haul and let go again,
his ankles braced with the pressure
into the angle of the wall, if once
then a dozen times, until the evil streak of liquid,
that slippery apodal anger, snaps clear,
is spat out by the fast shallow river
and its stonewashed Ophelias, and ascends writhing,
tying and untying itself like the bait on the barbs
clutching its slimy guts. Fearless,
the boy wrestles the shining hatred to the ground
to remove the immovable hook, making
the wild thing curl, squeeze and embrace,
like a long-lost forearm, his forearm, from genuine pain
or overt affection, in a lithe Celtic pattern,
a *fin-de-siècle* spiral, an ornate looping bracelet
that would stay with the youngster, the scar

from knuckles to elbow ready to spring to life
when he eats that flayed devil boiled with onions,
its vicious alien head imprinted on his palm.

AMADAN

To excuse Charlie Barr everything except what life
has dealt him, his mother took up with a thug his own age,
while his father (lackadaisical and little cared for)
died of causes unknown and dropped straight to hell.

But Charlie Barr stayed where he was and went supremely mad.
He forgot to shave and cultivated a limp after his lurid girlfriend
(thin and hard) kicked him out, took the child (not his),
deadlocked the door and stopped shouting long enough

for Charlie Barr to go nowhere with no one, just up
the town and down, dragging his heel and answering the voice
(not hers) by directing cars and kicking dogs, in a hurry
to get where he's going so he can start again, because

Charlie Barr enjoys it, as far as it goes; because it makes him
feel good, usually, all those times he catches sight of himself
in a shopfront before stoving it in with a boot or head butt
to the glass, himself as others see him, but in reverse.

SOMERVILLE

The air is still. Chlorophyll stifles goosegrass and nettles,
the great trees glowing above the low-water glitter ...
Suddenly a hawk is pinned and wriggling to the sky's blue breast,
and you can keep it in sight from the deranged bike
as you overtake the braless woman pushing a tireless baby
and bags of goods in a shopping trolley along the cycle path.
Nobody, least of all you, wants to be a freewheeler all their life.
The hawk drops as if winged, and a search party of cattle
fans out, intent on blood and feathers, so missing
the jet-glint break its connections to the infinite and plummet
to the fine line between heaven and hell ... You are heading
that way, easily by the shortest route, measuring time
by the beat of the pedals and space by the mangled butterflies,
leaving the consumerist pietà of mother and child
to the mercies of underpasses, defenceless playgrounds,
and the 'Lili Marlene' and 'Greensleeves' of the ice-cream van
when it goes visiting the cardboard houses in silent estates.

ASH

A year's impurities of lies and big promises –
the mind polluted – and things have changed,
the trick is changing them for the better.
On good days I won the battle of my weight,
and, knickerless, you shimmied into a tarty dress
that retold every nook and curve.

That was then, when there was everything to play for,
and this is now, in injury time, with the aftertaste
of a late sun like a kiss on the tongue,
and shoals of starlings scintillating against a moon-
slice in summery orbit, the sombre air fizzing
with wayward stars and ash, motes

from your leavings I haul to the bonfire
I put together (for this evening belongs to me) –
a godbotherer on land ripe for development –
shoes and toiletries, a double-sided mirror,
some bed linen, anything that smacks of you;
the piano taking time to burn,

to be played by the impatient flames
that familiar discordant, dissonant refrain
from the heat and light of argument. Inevitably,
the fire, once spotted, like a skip or a hole
in the ground, soon has everyone joining in
with bits and pieces, their own ifs, buts and maybes.

THE ONLY DARKNESS

Crowded jets and motorised bees swarm to Shannon.
Sight unseen, a compendium of Spanish hulks, holed
and heavy, halo the western coast with coinage.

In clover, Inishowen almost kisses the North, a castle
on its lips, waiting for cameras to reload, the Valencia Lates
having rolled free on the floor of the car,

rising and falling in first to a golden skelf of beach,
the Atlantic holding on by its fingernails
and flashing tawdry sequins as it swans the headlands

of a twisted geomorphology, alive this hour
with seventeen-year-old girls scorched with freckles,
lace tiaras over Alice bands, anoraks hiding nylon uniforms

that will comfort residents stung by tears and tides,
the only darkness some synthetic crows, the polished eye
of a heron gull, the waitresses' opaque tights.

PATTERN

Helicopters get high on the knowledge
that nothing has changed,
war, pestilence and famine;
phalanx after phalanx of haybales

making a stand with unbiddable crows
as the baler embroiders
the field of gold velour
with rabbit and domestic cat.

ON BEING ASKED DIRECTIONS TO DRUMCREE

by two hacks from a London broadsheet,
I lean into their foul Isuzu 4x4, all bull bars
and pocket phones, burger boxes and burnt stubs,
the black golf-ball compass floating helpless
on the dingy windscreen, and tell them
like everywhere else it's a long way from here.
I elaborate with hand signals, the driver
thumbnailing a map and making a note,
his passenger tapping the compass as if it were
the oracle, the lifesaver, as if it made
a button of difference here of all places,
after my parting shot point them
in the opposite direction to arrive
sometime tomorrow or the day after that.

WEEKENDERS

Seagulls are children. Their cries are lost
on us, and their moulded toys colour the lawn.

Skinny hail scrabbles the double glazing,
and the thin-skinned, ink-stained Atlantic

clutches at land impossible to get emptier,
in all directions the same storm-scorched folds

of the waitress's pinny.
You sneeze twice, and wait for the echo.

BALLYEDENORDINARY

In the middle of a walk to the middle of their lives
she says he doesn't love her: it's a question of commitment.
So familiar is the slalom of moleskin he can draw
its ups and downs in his head, momentum driving

his imagination to the circus tent in the middle ground
behind a shambolic nine-hole of par threes
(with pub attached) and a plethora of villages
like smashed headstones overlooked by high cloud.

No animals these days; just clowns and acrobats
and who in their right mind would want to see that?
Yes, it's a question of commitment. They stop
on the crest of the road, the court cairn keeping its secrets,

the land below now a cemetery resembling the past,
and him knowing in his heart of hearts
he was the man rumoured to be on the run
though everyone else knew he was not being chased.

MY ONLY UNCLE'S STORY

In a San Diego Chevrolet (ten miles on the clock) he found
his way to Nevada, intending to hit the Lakota reservations.
He had heard they do magic there, and talk to ghosts,
and that nothing had changed in Eureka since the gold dried up.
Only later was he told (by people he didn't know)
he had also found the loneliest highway in the States –
the 305, heading north. And certainly, once the cruise control
was engaged, he virtually flew over those badlands
until, after a blissful hour of nothingness, the first automobile
he met coming the opposite direction turned on a dime
and rolled its tumbling Spielberg lights into his mirrors.
The cop sauntered over, ordering my only uncle to stay in the car;
my only uncle did as he was told, and produced licence,

insurance and apologies through the open window: eighty-eight,
it transpired, wasn't legal, even for a blow-in guzzling the desert.
He thought of being in Rome, and promised, tongue-in-cheek,
whatever was needed to get back on the blacktop cleaving
those disgruntled giants blockading Aloysius O'Ford country.
The cop, of course, relented, and my only uncle put another
hundred miles between himself and sunset before he had to kick
the dust from his Goodyears. But he has the devil's luck,
and the following week was caught in California for the same offence,
and yet again let off by employing his now peanut-butter brogue.
I don't know how he got from there to Mexico but as he says himself,
'Those señoritas are out of this world!' That's what I mean:
he is restless and horny, and tells stories like they were gospel.

Or shouts them. Because he is going deaf and doesn't know he shouts –
part of that difference, that eerie way of coping with life's
nasty obligations like hangovers, obituaries, lies and divorce.
He is the skeleton in the family cupboard, the scapegoat
for all our ills who escaped because he could take no more,
and who, four times married, still dips a red rose in liquid gold
to the memory of the only woman he ever loved. He has lost two stone,
cultivated a ponytail, and can air guitar to Jerry Garcia blasting
from the dashboard of a monster car all his own. It whistles in fifth,
has been round the clock once already, and is streamlined
and thirsty enough to be a Yankee. And though he puts his deafness
to good use (a new girlfriend every six months), it's the car radio
sleeps beside him, and the only jewellery he wears is Apache.

WHAT MIGHT HAVE BEEN

So beautiful, she says, where Armagh meets Down –
wilder, greener, no roads visible, and no obvious join
or crease, no border seam or tripwire, no ditch or wall
or marker, and the fields remaining still like the politics

and where you can be alone if you want to. Beautiful,
I agree, but doubly so as she was with me, both of us
transformed and walking together for many miles
without meeting another soul until everything was ours.

ACKNOWLEDGEMENTS

Acknowledgements are due to the editors of the following publications:

Arvon Prize Winners' Anthology 1998, *Atlanta Review* (USA), *Big Spoon*, *Brangle*, *Burning Bush*, *Cencrastus*, *Fortnight*, *Honest Ulsterman*, *Magma*, *Metre*, *Other Poetry*, *Peterloo Poets Winners' Anthology 2002*, *Poetry Ireland Review*, *Poetry Review*, *Seam*, *Stand*, *Staple*, *Tabla*, *Chiron Review* (USA), *Edinburgh Review*, *The Frogmore Papers*, *The North*, THE SHOp, TLS, *Turret Books Broadsheet 1998*.

I also wish to thank the Old Museum Arts Centre (OMAC) in Belfast and the Verbal Arts Centre in Derry.